Android Crash Course

By: PG WIZARD BOOKS

Step by Step Guide To Mastering Android Programming!

Android Crash Course: Step by Step Guide To Mastering Android
Programming!

Table of Contents

Introduction

Working with the Android operating system can be a great experience. Unlike some of the other coding languages and operating systems out there, Android is the language that you will work with for mobile devices rather than for your computer. With that being said, you are still able to work on the computer, using an emulator, so that you can check out if the app that you create is going to work properly or not.

If you are interested in creating some of your own apps with the help of the Android operating system, this is the guidebook that is going to help you to get it done. It is a simple program to learn how to use, and this guidebook is going to make it easier than ever to get started. We will talk about some of the basics of working with the Android operating system as well as how it is all set up for you to use. Once that is done, we are going to learn how to download the Android operating system, set up the emulator, write your first code, and even make some changes to it later on. There is so much that you are able to do with the help of this operating system and we are going to take a look at some of the best parts of it with this guidebook.

When you are ready to learn a new coding language for your mobile devices, and you want to be able to create some of your own applications, make sure to check out this guidebook for the basics on how to get started from doing updates, to installing the software and even creating some of your first programs.

Chapter 1: An Overview of Android

If you are someone who likes to work in programming and even on smartphones, then the Android operating system is a great option for you to use. Android is an operating system that is based off Linux, which makes it really easy for you to use. The user interface is considered as direct manipulation based and it is one that will be used and designed to work with tablets and smartphones that are touchscreens as well as cars, televisions, and wristwatches that are compatible with this technology. With the operating system, you are able to make use of the touch inputs which will be able to correspond with actions that are done in the real world, such as pinching, swiping, and tapping.

With all of the things that Android is able to work with, you are going to find many different projects that you are able to create. Android is a really low-cost operating system that is ready made and can be customized to the needs that you have. And since it is able to be used with other high-tech devices, it has become really popular with a wide range of technology companies. Add in that this is an open source operating system (which means that programmers are able to use it and make changes as they see fit), it is easy to use on your own projects, and you can even find a large community of developers who can help you out.

There are many features that you are going to find with the Android system. You will be able to use it with other languages to work on your device, it has the power that you need to compete with the Apple operating system and Windows 8.1 it is able to store all the information that you need, works with your Wi-Fi, and even has an interface that is intuitive for the user. These are some of the features that you can enjoy while using the Android operating system and with the new innovations that are always coming out thanks to this code being open sourced, you are sure to find other benefits that will help you to get your projects done.

Android is one of the best-operating systems out there for devices like tablets, televisions, and mobile phones. There are billions of these devices hooked up to the Android system, and it has quickly become one of the largest mobile platform bases with a huge growth potential in the future. In fact, according to the Google Corporation, it is believed that more than a million new devices are activated with Android each day.

Android Crash Course: Step by Step Guide To Mastering Android Programming!

The interface

By default, the user interface in Android is going to be base don the touch inputs of the user with options like pinching, swiping, and tapping on the objects, or the keyboard on the screen of the device. So basically this is an operating system that is designed to respond to the input of the user right away, and it includes a smooth touch interface to make things easier. You will also find that this operating system is going to put to use the vibration feature of the device, so the user is able to get some haptic feedback.

The internal hardware that comes with this operating system, such as accelerometers, gyroscopes, and proximity sensors are used by the applications, and you can use it for adjusting the orientation of the screen, using remote controls, and even change up the home screen for the different pages that you use. Basically, this is a very intuitive interface that the user is going to love because it responds to their touches and it has so many different options that they are able to use.

Managing the memory

For the most part, the devices that run on Android are going to use battery. So if you want to make sure that the battery life is going to last longer, you will want to have a RAM that will consume less power because they will not get a continuous source of power like some of your desktop devices. Whenever the app is minimized, or it isn't in use, it is going to be placed inside the memory automatically. Yes, these applications are going to be open still, but this method is going to help to prevent it from consuming all the resources of the system; they will simply wait in the background until you decide to call them back up.

This is great for the Android device because you will be able to call it back up as needed, but it helps to save the limited RAM that you have. The RAM is limited because you want to make sure that it doesn't waste out all the battery power that you have this device. Luckily, this system is going to be good at managing some of your applications. If it notices that your memory is running low, it is simply going to terminate the processes that aren't being used, closing up the oldest applications first to save room.

Android Crash Course: Step by Step Guide To Mastering Android
Programming!

Security and privacy

Many people are worried about getting on a new operating system is whether it is going to keep your privacy safe and if it is secure enough to work on the apps with. There are many operating systems that promise to be amazing when it comes to your security and privacy, but some of them may fall short at some times and won't provide the benefits that you are looking for. But when it comes to the Android operating system, you are going to get all the benefits of a lot of security and privacy, simply by the way that the system is set up to deal with the work that you are doing and since you get to determine how all the apps interact on the computer and get to give each of them permission before they get any information, you know that your privacy is always going to be safe.

The applications that you use in Android are going to run inside the sandbox, which is basically an area of your system that is isolated and will not have access to the other resources unless you give permission for this when you install the application. Before you install a new application, you will also need to give permission in order to get it on the system. This is going to take a bit more time through the installation process, but it helps to prevent bugs in the applications, limits documentation, and helps to keep your information secure and private no matter what.

Works with different languages

One of the nice things about working with the Android operating system is that it is able to work with many other coding languages. Almost all of the major coding languages are supported on these devices, and the list is currently at over 100 languages. This makes it easy for the Android device to adapt to what you want to use. It also supports Java so that if you want to create something to work online, the Java language is going to be easy to use.

These are just some of the things that you are going to fall in love with when you get started on the Android platform. It is great to work with mobile devices, no matter what kind you have, it has a lot of speed and stability so that you know that your coding will work out well, and you can develop many different kinds of applications, in many different coding languages if you want, without too much hassle.

The benefits of working with the Android operating system

Android Crash Course: Step by Step Guide To Mastering Android
Programming!

When it comes to working with an operating system that works out well with your mobile devices, none of them are going to be as great as the Android operating system. There are other options, but the Android operating system is going to work on billions of devices all over the world. Some of the benefits that you will be able to enjoy with this operating system include:

- Easy to use: working with the Android operating system can be really easy. You are going to learn how to create some of your own apps in no time, and then you can bring out your own creativity to work with Android or to create the apps that you dream about.
- Works well with mobile devices: the whole idea of using the Android operating system is so that you are able to use it to create apps that are good for your mobile devices. This can include things like televisions, tablets, and smartphones. You can use the emulator that is available for your computer, or your own device, in order to create an app and then have a chance to try it out to see if it works.
- Works with the Java language: you will need to know how to work with the Java language if you want to work on an Android app. This is a basic website and online building language that is easy to use, but it is important that you learn how to use this ahead of time.
- Allows you to create and sell your own apps: one of the reasons that a lot of people will choose to go with the Android operating system is because they have some ideas for apps that they want to use and hope to sell. There are millions of people who use the Android operating system on their devices, and they are always looking for new apps and games to work with. Some people choose to sell the apps for free, and others will make money off of the added space they sell or the cost of the app. This is a great way to make some extra money if you like to work with apps.
- The user interface is easy to work with: this user interface is meant to be really interactive. In fact, it is going to work mainly by the user working with their hands and fingers rather than relying on buttons and clicks like the other operating systems that you may be used to. This can make it easier for you to learn how to make apps that the customer will love because they can work on it in real time without all the extras going on around it causing it to be slower.
- A big community to ask questions with: the Android system has a big community of people you are able to meet with, ask questions of, and so much more when you need help. Android has been around for a long time,

and it has a lot of devices that will use this system to get things done. This makes it easier for you to use the operating system and to get it to work the way that you would like.

There are many options that you can choose when it comes to making a mobile operating system work for your app. Some people will use the Windows system and other times you will want to go with the Apple iOS. But none have the wide range and all the flexibility that you need from the Android operating system, and this is why so many people choose to go with it. With billions of devices that use this operating system and a million more being added each day, it is no wonder that people love being able to use and learn how to use Android.

Chapter 2: The Architecture of the Android Operating System

Before we get too far into developing our programs with the Android operating system, it is important to know some of the architecture that comes with this program and where things will work together. The framework of the application is easier to understand if we know how things are going to be arranged and will work inside of the operating systems. Since this is an operating system that is based on Linux, you will see that the two are very similar if you have worked with Linux in the past. For those who have never worked on Linux at all, you will notice that the layout of the language is pretty simple to use and you will catch on pretty quickly. Let's take a look at the architecture of this operating system.

Basic applications

The first applications that you are going to see are the basic ones. These are some of the options like the application to make calls, for your music player and camera and more. They don't have to come from Google, and sometimes Google isn't going to provide them at all, but you will be able to use the Google play store in order to develop these kinds of applications and make it so that they are available for everyone to use. You can also develop the apps with Java and then install them into the device that will integrate with the Android operating system.

Application framework

This is the part of the system that is going to be used for developing the applications. This framework is available with many different interfaces, and the developers will pick out which interface they want to use based on the standards that are important to them. By using these frameworks, you are going to save a lot of time and effort because it is not necessary to code out all of the tasks. There are also some different entities that come with the framework, and the options available are going to change based on the framework that you want to use.

Activity manager

Android Crash Course: Step by Step Guide To Mastering Android
Programming!

When you are using the activity manager, you are using the part of the program that is responsible for managing the different activities that control the app life cycle. It is going to have many different states, and the activity manager will be able to handle all of these. The applications are going to consist of many different types of activities, and each of these activities is going to have its own life cycle. Whenever you launch up a new application, one main activity is going to be started. You will be able to pull up a window when needed in order to see every activity inside an app.

Resource managers

If you have some applications that are going to require some kind of external resources, such as an external string, these are going to be managed with the help of your resource manager. These parts are going to be able to allocate the resources in the way that is standard for your device and will make sure that everything works together well.

Libraries

There are several libraries that you are able to us in Android in order to make sure that you are using the right codes, to save time, and to make your work more powerful. All of the native libraries for Android are going to be found inside of this layer, but all of them are going to be written using either the C++ or the C language. The capabilities that are found inside these libraries are going to be similar to what you find in the application layer on the top of the Linux kernel. Some of the things that you are going to find inside of these libraries on Android will include:

- Surface manager: this is the compositing window in manager and display.
- System C libraries: these are the basic libraries of C that are going to be targeted for the ARM or embedded devices.
- A media framework: this could include options for playback, recording, video, audio, and more.
- OpenGL ES libraries: this is the one that is needed for the graphics on the device.

- SQLite: this is a database engine. This one, in particular, is a smaller version that works better on Android without using up as much memory space.

All of these are going to come together in order to help you to find out the codes that you would like to use inside your program. You can use these as a simple way to get started on the app that you would like to use or as some suggestions as to what you would need to do next. You can always add in some of the other parts that you would like if the code really needs it, but this is one of the best places to start as a beginner in order to get your basics down and to start writing some of your own code.

Android Runtime

You will find that the Dalvik Virtual Machine is the part that is in charge of the runtime for all Android devices. This is a virtual machine that is going to be used for your embedded devices as well as an interpreter for bytecode. They are going to have lower memories and can be a bit slower than you are used to since they run on batteries. You will find that the Java libraries are also going to be on these devices which means that you will be able to use them.

Kernel

When it comes to using the Android operating system, you will be using the Linux Kernel 2.6. This is going to include all the electronic equipment that you need, and many of the processes are going to be similar to what you will find with the Linux operating system to make things easier. Between the software and hardware of Android, you are going to see that the kernel will behave similar to the abstraction layer in the hardware and will include essential parts like the keypad, camera, and display. The kernel is also going to be in charge of handling things like the networking and device drivers.

Keep in mind that working with the Linux system means that everything is going to be in the form of a kernel. This helps to add in some security to the system and makes the whole program easier to use. If you have ever worked with the Linux system, you are used to how easy the Linux operating system is to do a lot of different tasks, and this is going to translate over to the work that you are doing over on the Android operating system as well.

Android Crash Course: Step by Step Guide To Mastering Android
Programming!

Now that you know a bit more about the different parts that come with the
Android operating system and how it does work quite well with the Linux system,
it is time to move on to downloading this software properly and working on a few
of your very first projects to make things easier.

Chapter 3: Working on Your First Project

Now that we have taken the time to learn more about the Android system, it is time to work on our first project. This one is going to be pretty simple to learn, but will help you to get a feel for how all of this works for some of the other topics we will bring up later on. But the first step that we need to take when getting started is to install the Android Studio.

To start with this, we need to see if the Java Development Kit, or the JDK, is installed on your computer or not. Some computers come with this already in place so that can save you time. For a PC, you need to click on Start, Run, type in the word "cmd" and then press enter to see if it is there. If you are on a Mac computer, you will use the Spotlight to search for the Terminal and then choose the top result. If this is on the computer, use the prompt "java-version." If a command is not found, you will need to visit the Oracle website and download the JDK on your computer.

Once this is done, it is time to go online and download the right version of the Android Studio for your computer. When this has had time to download the right way on the computer, you can click on Next to move on to the following screen. At this location, you will need to pick the setup that you want to use (standard is usually the best one) before clicking on Next and accepting the license agreements. At this point, the Android Studio is going to finish up the download, and you are ready.

For each version of Android that you are using, you will find that it contains a version of SDK for you to work with. The setup wizard is going to help you to get the updated versions of this. It is important to have the SDK because it helps you to set up the Android Virtual Device, the part that allows you to test your new apps on it and you can give it the right customizations for your own personal configuration.

So go back to the Welcome Screen of the Android Studio and click Configure. You should see a new menu that offers you a lot of options, and you will want to pick the one that says SDK Manager. A new window should appear when you click on this, and a series of folders, checkboxes, and statuses are going to show up. If you just downloaded the Android Studio, you should have the latest version of SDK

Tools as well as some of the other tools to make the program work. If you see that an update is still available for this, the box will be ticked, and you can choose whether or not you want to take this.

Once you have had time to get the latest version of the SDK Manager on your computer (taking the time to update it if you need), it is time to create one of your first programs inside of the Android operating system.

Creating the OMG Android

Now it is time to start working on your very first project, and we are going to start out pretty simple, using the Hello, World! Kind of idea that the other coding languages go with. The idea behind this one is to give you some options and familiarity with using Android so that you can do some of the bigger projects later on.

The nice thing that you will notice about the Android Studio is that it comes with a nice tool that will give you the steps that you need to get this project started. You will just need to get on the Welcome Screen, click that you want to start a New Android Studio Project, and then the screen for project creation will show up. You are allowed to place an application name, and we are going to call this one OMG Android. For the company domain just put in your name. You may notice that the Package Name is going to change at this time to make a reverse domain name based on what you call the application and your company. This is going to be like a unique identifier so that the app is easily found among all the others.

Set the project location to the hard drive location that you would like before clicking on Next. On this screen, you are going to tell the system which devices and operating systems you would like to make the app work with. You probably don't want to make an app that will work with each Android device, but you can narrow this down to just smartphones or just tablets if you would like. For this one, to keep things easier, we are going to target the Android phone (you should see that this is the default option selected along with the Minimum SDK).

You can then click on Next to get to the following screen to choose what activity will happen for the app. A good way to think about this is as a window inside the

15

app that will be able to show what content will be interactive with the user. You can use this activity as a popup or as the while window. Inside of this template, the activities are going to range from being blank with an Action Bar all the way to one that has an embedded Map View. But for this project, we are going to keep things simple and work with Blank Activity before clicking Next.

At this point, you are almost to the coding. We are going to go through and use the default options with this and then click on the Finish button. There will be a few minutes for the Studio to go through and finish off the project and sometimes you will notice that it is going through all the different steps and putting out information about what it is doing. The nice thing is that with this IDE, a lot of work is going to be done for you.

After a few minutes, the Studio is going to finish building up this project. This project so far is going to be empty since we didn't put in any code to it, but it will contain all the information that is needed to be launched on one of the Android devices. At this point, you should see that there are three windows that are open on the Android Studio. On the left is going to be the project folder, the middle will have a preview of what this looks like on the Nexus 5, and then the last window is going to show the layout of the project.

Right now the project is pretty empty and will not show much up on the screen, but you will be able to make changes to that later on and add in some words as well as some other really cool things. But for now, you have created a good program so let's take that a step further in the next chapter and not only add in some of the words or phrases that you need to work with inside this operating system, but also learn how to make the app run with your emulator or with the Android   device.

Chapter 4: Running the App

So in the last chapter, we spent some time making a pretty basic app. We learned
how to get it all setup and that the Android Studio is really great at setting the
defaults that you want to use and which will ensure that you have it named the
right way and ready to go. But so far the app doesn't have any words in it for
others to see or any other actions, and it isn't running in a way that the other
Android apps will be able to use. This chapter is going to take some time to add in
these two options so that you can make your app start to work.

Running the app on an Emulator

So with the example that we did in the previous chapter, we took the time to
create our first app, but now we need to figure out how to run that. If you already
own an Android device, you are able to use this to run and test out the app, but if
you don't have a device, you can choose to work with an emulator. The Android
Studio is going to include the abilities that you need to set up a software-based
device right on your computer. This basically means that you can run apps, debut
the app, and look through a website on your computer, but it will work as if you
were on the Android app. You will be able to set up as many emulators on your
computer, and you can mess around with the screen size, version of the platform,
and more to really see how the app is going to work.

If you went through the setup wizard properly on the last steps, you could already
have the emulator in place on your computer. But we are going to take a moment
to set up a brand new emulator in case you missed this option before or if you
would like to choose a second emulator on the computer.

To get started on this is to click on the AVD Manager. You should be able to look
inside of the toolbar for the icon that has the Android popping up and is beside a
device with a purple display. The Android Studio is going to have one of these
setups that you are able to use, and you will be able to see some details about the
type of the emulator, the API that it uses, and the CPU instructions.

Android Crash Course: Step by Step Guide To Mastering Android
Programming!

But if you would like to create a brand new AVD, you will just need to click on the Create Virtual Device. Now you will need to come up with some choices. For the first one, you will need to decide which device you would like to emulate. You should be able to look over to the left and see a list of categories that basically list all of the devices that you will be able to emulate and then you can see the different devices in each category. To make things simple, we are going to click on the Phone category and choose the Nexus S. once you pick this one, click on the Next.

Now you also need to decide on the Android version you would like to use. There are a few options that are available, and we are going to pick one of them, Lollipop. Check that when you are on this that the ABI column shows a value of x86 to ensure that the emulator is going to run at a good speed. Click on the Next button. This page should basically be a confirmation screen that you should double check before clicking on Finish and ending this process.

At this point, you have created a brand new virtual device that will allow you to test out your app. You should close down the AVD Manager and then head back to your main screen of the Android Studio. For the final step, you will click on Run before another window shows up and you can choose which device you want to test this app on. You shouldn't have any of the devices running here so you can start with the AVD that you created earlier, just make sure to click on the Launch Emulator and that the AVD is selected before clicking on OK.

Here you will need to give the emulator some time to load up, and you may even need to do this a few times to get it right. Once all of this is loaded properly, you will be able to see what there is of the running app.

So now that this emulator is all set up, it is time to add a bit more to the code that we did earlier so that we can see how it is going to work on other Android devices. We are going to keep this one simple right now, but you can always expand on this to get more out of it. So to start on this, you will need to go to res/values/strings.xml and then double click on this file. We are going to change this so that we can make it a bit more personal and have some fun with it. Here is the syntax of what you should type in:

<string name = "hello_world">I am learning Android!

</string>

You would be able to change up the code to say anything that you would like
inside of this part of the code, making the string a lot longer, changing up the
message, and so much more. This is just a great little way of showing how the
code can work. But with this one, you have created your first app and even made
some changes to make it a bit more personalized. You will just need to click on
Run when it is done, and the message that you wrote out should show up on the
screen.

Chapter 5: Doing Updates with the SDK Manager

Now we are going to take some time to do a bit more with the app that you want
to create. This is all going to work regardless of the version of SDK that you would
download on your computer so even if one of the older versions is there; it will
still work. If you would like to make sure to open up the SDK Manager from
inside the project, you will just need to click on the button that has the downward
arrow with your Android peeking above it. When we are done with this section,
we are going to be able to make a lot of changes to the app, and we will have one
that has a PNG image, has an editable text field, and so much more.

So at this point, we need to have our "Hello, World!" app open and ready to go on
the device, or you can use the emulator if that is the method that you would like
to work with so that the message is showing. But now it is time to take this over to
the next level.

Getting started on this project

For this one, we are going to take a moment to look ahead. The first thing that
you will want to do with this step of the project is to make sure that the app is
going to be simple. You don't want to add in a lot of complexities at this part
because this can slow down the app, introduces some more bugs to the system,
and just makes it more difficult for the user to work with. You only want to add in
extra parts if you really need it for the app to work properly, but right now this is
going to take some more time and work than what we want to work with at the
time.

So to get started, we are going to need to open up the
app/res/layout/activity_main.xml. If you are able to see the .raw and .xml file,
you will be good to go. But if this is not showing up, you will need to go to the
bottom of your screen and see if you need to switch all of this over to the Text
mode. All we will do at this point is work to get rid of some of the attributes that
are just padding to it. The Studio often adds these things to the .xml file on its
own, but it can make it harder to work on the file. You are going to want to look
for and delete all of these lines before we continue:

android:paddingLeft="@dimen/activity_horizontal_margin

android:paddingRight=@dimen/activity_horizontal_margin

android:paddingTop=@dimen/activity_vertical_margin

android:paddingBottom=@dimen/activity_vertical_margin

If you went through all of this and did it the proper way, your new .xml file is
going to look like the following:

```
<RelativeLayout

xmlns:android=http://schemas.android.com/apk/res/android

xmlns:tools=http://schemas.android.com/tools

android:layout_width="match_parent"

android:layout_height="match_parent"

tools:context=".MainActivity">


<TextView

android:text="@string/hello_world

android:layout_width="wrap_content"

android:layout_height="wrap_content"/>


</RelativeLayout>
```

At this point, we will need to look for the Mainactivity.java part of the code. You
will need to look on the left pane that is inside of Studio and then double click on
it. We are going to take a moment to look at the very first piece of code, and you
will need to move out a few of the lines including the following:

```
@Override

public boolean onOptionsItemSelected(MenuItem item){
```

//Handle action bar item clicks here. The action bar will

//automatically handle clicks on the Home/Up button, so long

//as you specify a parent activity in AndroidManifest.xml.

int id = item.getItemId();

//noinspection SimplifiableIfStatement

if (id == R.id.action_settings){

return true;

}

return super.onOptionsItemSelected(item);

}

You should be careful when you are doing this to make sure that you are leaving the final curly brace in its place when you delete the other options. This is the curly brace that is going to close up your class ahead of it, and you want to make sure that it is still there. Now that all the housekeeping work has been done, it is time to get to work and give the Activity a new life of its own.

Chapter 6: How to Publish Your Android App

Now that we have had some time to create our own app a little bit and learn how to manage the app in a way that makes it have less stuff in the way and so that it does more of the work that you want, it is time to learn how to publish your own app. You are going to work with making a lot of different types of apps over the years when you get familiar with working with the Android operating system and it is likely that you will at some point want to be able to publish one of the apps to make some money or for other people to be able to use it as well. In this chapter, we are going to spend some time learning how to take one of the apps that you create and getting it published.

The first thing to know is that when creating an Android app, you will need to publish it on the Google Play store. This means that you will need to create your own account using the Google Play Developer Console. This account is going to cost a little bit of money to create, about $25 at the publishing of this book, but considering the other parts of the operating system are free, this isn't so bad. The reason that there are fees with this account is that the Google company wants to keep out people who would make duplicate or fake accounts and helps to avoid people flooding the store with bad apps that no one else wants.

After you have gone through and created the account and paid the beginning fees, you are going to have your own Google Play Developer Account. You will be able to choose as many apps as you would like to publish on this account and you can choose whether you would like to publish those apps for free for others to use or in a manner to make money through the system. Some people are turned away by the fees, but if you are looking to make some money with this system on your apps by selling them, you will find that you can quickly make this $25 back. You can also allow ads to be on your app and earn some ad-revenue if you would like.

So to get this started, you just need to visit the site https://developer.android.com/distribute/index.html. Then you will just need to follow the steps that come up on the prompts to help you figure out what you are supposed to do to finish the account. In the end, you will finish creating your own developer account, pay the fees that are associated with the account to get it started, and then complete the process.

Android Crash Course: Step by Step Guide To Mastering Android Programming!

At this point, you are probably done with creating your append are ready to upload it into the system. You will just need to upload the app file in a manner that is similar to how you would attach a link or a document into your email. Then you will be asked to take a survey. This is not something that you will be able to skip out on because the system wants to know about the different factors and features about your app. Some of the questions that it is going to ask is about whether there are inappropriate contents inside and if there are any age restrictions on using the app.

After you are done with setting up your account and getting the app to upload inside of the program, you are going to need to give Google a few days in order to validate the app. You will be able to add in as many of these apps as you would like over time, but you still need to give it a few days before it is going to show up inside the app store.

And that is all that you would need to do in order to get the app to work inside of the Google Play Store. You will be able to choose to offer the game for free, add some ad revenue into the system to make money, or charge for people to use the app in the first place. There are many options about the type of apps that you are able to use, and since it is so easy to add it to the Google store, you will be able to develop the app, get it put up, and move on to the next project in no time.

Conclusion

The Android operating system is a great one for you to learn how to use whenever you are looking to create an app or another program that works on phones, tablets, televisions and other mobile options. It is based on the Linux system which makes it easy to learn how to use (especially if you already know how to use this system), and you will find that over 100 coding languages are recognized on Android, so you are able to pick the one that is best for you.

In this guidebook, we took some time to look at the different parts of the Android operating system. We started out with some of the basics of this system before moving on to how set up the architecture that is inside of the code, how to create one of your own programs, and even how to set up an emulator so that you can run the code on your computer (which can be nice if you don't have a specific Android device around) and see how it is going to work for you.

There is so much to love with the Android operating system. With billions of devices around the world using this system for making apps or running the programs that they want on their mobile devices, it is easy to learn how to use this operating system for developing your own apps or for your own personal use. Use this guidebook to learn more about how the Android operating system works and to make it create the best programs for you..

www.ingramcontent.com/pod-product-compliance
Lightning Source LLC
LaVergne TN
LVHW052319060326
832902LV00021B/3985